My Canadian Journey

My First 2 Years as an Immigrant and Starting Over in Canada

OLIVIA R. NANSUBUGA

Copyright © 2023 Olivia R. Nansubuga

All rights reserved. This publication, or any part thereof, may not be reproduced in any form, or by any means, including electronic, photographic, or mechanical, or by any sound recording system, or by any device for storage and retrieval of information, without the written permission of the copyright owner.

Second Edition: April 2023

ISBN: 978-0-9842170-6-9

My Canadian Journey: My First 2 Years as an Immigrant and Starting Over in Canada/ Olivia R. Nansubuga

Publisher: MAWMedia Group, LLC
Los Angeles | Reno | Nashville

Dedication

I would like to appreciate the following people that helped me along this wonderful two years' journey:

First, my sincere gratitude goes to the Government of Canada and the Canadian people at large. I felt the love, compassion, and kindness which stems from a true Canadian culture. The support that I got through the systems that the government put in place for newcomers and immigrants was essential for the successful navigation of my journey.

Thank you, Right Hon. Ambassador Joy Ruth, Reverand Pastors Mr & Mrs Jackie and Joseph Kiirya , Mr & Mrs Sseggiriinya, Ms. Betty, Ms. Doreen, Ms. Sarah, Andrew, Collins, ~~Sarah~~, my employer John, and my first clients-the Holly family.

Table of Contents

Dedication 5
Table of Contents 6
Prologue 7
Section I: Arriving in a New Land 13
Chapter 1: Arriving in Canada 14
Chapter 2: Ottawa 21
Section II: Living and Surviving 26
Chapter 3: Shelter 27
Chapter 4: Driving 36
Section III: The Lessons to Send Back Home 43
Chapter 6: Systems Knowledge 44
Chapter 7: Mental Habits 50
Chapter 8: Behavioral Habits 54
Chapter 9: Learning Orientation 58
Chapter 10: Self-Sufficiency 61

Prologue

You make a life out of what you have, not what you are missing.
Kate Morton

Hello readers: Thank you for choosing my book to guide you to success on your immigration journey. For anyone planning to immigrate to a country they have never been (or to be specific, Canada), for anyone who is already in that new country, and you sometimes feel alone, stuck, lost, hopeless, or low, I want to tell you that you are not alone; I have been there. I hope you find inspiration in this easy-to-read book about my two years journey as an immigrant in Canada.

If you are not planning to immigrate anytime soon and find yourself reading my book, don't close it yet; there is something for you. Vera Nazarian once said, "Whenever you read a good book, somewhere in the world, a door opens to allow in more light." I believe that my journey's experience shared here will ignite the fire to pursue your dreams and be fulfilled with your success.

Every immigration story is unique. It begins in your home country. You manage two processes—that of your home country (preparing physically, mentally, and financially) and that of the host country. The determinants of each case ruling are not obvious, just like we can't tell how the judge will decide one's case in the court hearing. One person may tell you that their process was 2 months. Another may tell you 5 years.

Starting Over

In education, relationships, and more, my life began again in Canada. I had to engage a new career. I had to build a new circle of friends. A journey into an unknown land can be intimidating. Merely thinking of the "how" is daunting. So many questions come to your mind and may create fears. How will I navigate the process? How will I get a visa? How do I start? This is why I share with my valued readers a personal story of my first two years. My experience may serve as your guide.

This book is organized into 3 sections, Arriving, Living & Surviving, and Lessons to Send Back Home. The following is an explanation of the goals and my reflections on each of the sections. I offer them to support your learning and experience while reading.

Arriving

As I have mentioned, this is an easy-to-read, raw story based on my own experience, told in my own simple words. You may have several emotions upon arrival. Own them with the recognition that this journey can be one of the most profound and beneficial of your life.

I had plans and aspirations for a better life. The minute I arrived, I felt that I was breathing a breath of fresh air. I was in a completely new land. I then noticed that the fresh air was chilly and cold. But that did not dampen my euphoria for the hope and faith that I held. I knew in that moment that I had taken the largest step toward my success contrary to the limitations I faced at home.

Living & Surviving

The government helps with some aspects of living and surviving. The greatest aspects of living are lessons that I present later, but the technical aspects like driving, housing, and obtaining a career, or getting confirmed in the country are practical elements you must consider.

Much of my initial concerns deal with money. Creating the opportunity to thrive will go through starting points with what you already know. Work with what you have. You do not need to go to school or gain certifications before you apply your skills to make money. The qualifications from back home will not suffice in many of the professions you had back home. More school may be required, but do not allow that to hinder you from making a living while you work toward certifications, degrees, or equivalencies. Refuse to look down on a job thinking it is beneath you.

Lessons to Send Back Home

In this book, I share my personal winning principles and

tips; the things that I did, how I did them, and how they helped me move forward through every step of my journey. Consider that life is more than making to the place. Surviving the journey is a beginning aspiration, but that has no satisfaction. Thriving is the goal. You do not accomplish these through striving. You accomplish through your personal growth.

The principles were in my mind. I had learned them on my own throughout my life. The immigration process allowed me to apply those principles to create the life I wanted. You will experience them differently for sure, but this is a starting point for you to consider. These offer a foundation to spur your courage and support you through your journey.

Goals are not set to achieve them. You achieve them at the end, but the journey of growth required is the point of goal setting. The steps that you take stimulate your growth as a person. I grow every day. My routine of gratitude and self-care support a level of growth that enables celebration throughout the journey. Once you get to the top of one mountain, you can enjoy the view and look forward to enjoying the journey more on the next mountain. You begin to realize that enjoying the journey is your success.

So, let's get started.

Section I: Arriving in a New Land

Chapter 1: Arriving in Canada

I began my journey in the 'Pearl of Africa' Uganda on January 28th, 2020. Sir Winston Churchill named the area in his 1908 book *My African Journey*. I am not really open with the reasons for leaving, but I am still healing from those experiences. Perhaps I will write them in detail in a memoir. Suffice it to say that life was not an experience of contentment. I desperately sought a way to make ends meet on my own. I was a captive of circumstances with the desire for independence. I wanted to experience financial freedom, do the things that interest me, make my own decisions, and improve my whole self.

I always wanted to be a person at the head, not the tail end. During my early years ~~When I was~~ in school, others saw the leadership gift within me. I did not see it myself. They pushed me even through my discomfort. I accepted and began to see my potential in small groups and other opportunities. I would take initiative rather than waiting for people to do things for me. I accepted my momentum and my status as a leader.

I noticed in my relationships that I was taking care of people though they were not taking care of me. I am the type of person who requires reciprocity in relationships. For me, those boundaries feel like personal qualities that reveal a lot about me. That may not seem intimate in other countries, but the structure of interactions is personal for me. I know that I am worth more than the minimum. I was willing to start over from scratch more than once to reach the experience of life that I deserve.

Even with my strong sense of boundaries and reciprocity, I continue to wrestle with the fear of being judged. I don't want people to think that I was a person that made poor choices. From the outside, I had a life in Uganda that a woman would love to have. I was to be envied. But I was not happy. I was not contented. I was engaged as a whole person seeking to have love, children, and contentment. That was not occurring, and I determined that I would seek more for my life. I wanted to stand on my own two feet according to my own standards not the standards of others. I needed to grow as a person, not just grow within the confines of my culture. My closest family and friends understood the struggle well. I am thankful for them.

Bon Voyage

This was not my first flight. I was familiar with airport formalities and experienced with at least 3 flights logged. I was always excited about flying. If someone was to tell me that I was going somewhere, I was the child who would sleep in their travel clothes and shoes to make sure I would not miss a moment. It's the love for adventure in me, the anticipation is always high.

I arrived early and met with my airport former colleagues. I knew I was packed expertly. I was confident that my journey would be pleasant because it was what I had set in my mind. I was looking forward to checking in and

My Canadian Journey

getting on to the plane. The process of clearing airport formalities went well, and shortly, we were airborne. This would be the longest flight I would take.

Eight hours and 15 minutes, and I did not close my eyes for once. I watched movies and read a book. I looked out the window as we crossed the Sahara Desert and other landmarks. I looked forward to experiencing something new. It was not only a releasing from my former life, but it was also anticipation of the certain success I would have. I knew it was a different place, and the comparison made the novel place "perfect." The buildings, the roads, the city lights, everything offered opportunity and beauty for me.

We landed at Schiphol airport, Netherlands. I had a good time there; I went window shopping in the duty-free shops, and I also met a long-time friend who was my former customer service supervisor while I worked at Entebbe airport.

I soon boarded my next plane, and in about 8 hours and 5 minutes, we landed at Toronto Pearson International

Airport at about 1700hrs on January 29th, 2020. It looked dark already, but understandably, it was wintertime when the days are shorter than the nights.

I disembarked the airplane, but I wasn't sure I knew which way to go, so I went with the flow of passengers and got to the conveyor belt to pick up my suitcase.

As I was waiting for my suitcase to arrive, I was praying that it would be taxied out of the baggage carousel and not be missing. My experience as an airport customer service agent somehow took me back to a time when I used to help passengers who couldn't find their bags because they were either delayed (to be loaded onto a later flight) or misrouted (loaded to a wrong destination). My suitcase finally came through. I had securely wrapped it at 'wrap and fly' a bag wrapping service at my check-in station, Entebbe. I also attached a yellow ribbon for easy identification in the event of a bag switch where passengers accidentally take other passengers' bags.

I then went straight ahead to clear my bag through

customs at the first entry port into Canada (in this case, Toronto), just like I was advised at check-in. After that, I would have it transferred to the next flight for my destination. My former job experience somehow helped me navigate the airport dynamics, I used to advise my passengers about some simple things to put in mind while travelling, especially for first-time travelers, and this time, it was my turn as I was on the receiving end though I had travelled several times before. The queue at the customs clearance was too long, and I was thinking of the little time I had to connect to my next flight.

When I got to the customs agent, she was very polite; she asked me a few questions regarding the contents of my bag and why I had come to Canada. She cleared me, and then I proceeded to drop off my bag to be loaded for my next flight. I continued to the self-check-in booth for clearance as she had advised me, then waited in the lounge for my next flight to Ottawa, my destination. At that point, I was hungry so, I spent the only money I had (USD 10). I bought potato chips and fruit juice according to my budget. The flight was soon ready, and I boarded.

Chapter 2: Ottawa

In about 2 hours, I was at Ottawa airport. A reasonable person would ask why Ottawa. My story begins with "Why not Toronto?" Toronto seemed too busy for me. I have heard that the cost of living was much higher than the City I settled in. I prefer the laid-back experience of Ottawa. It is obviously more family friendly. The slow pace and quiet is a solid foundation for peace.

Ottawa is the administrative center of the country. The parliament meets here. The prime minister's residence is here. Every province has its provincial governance, but this is the seat of the country's government apparatus. I can't compare it to other cities, but I can say that Ottawa is easy to fall in love with.

Most important for me are the opportunities. The pattern back home is one of struggle after college. Ottawa presents several employment opportunities for those with a work permit. Volunteer work is another option and a mandatory value in Canada. Social workers are invaluable in helping you find options. They will also connect you with legal aid. More about that when I share that experience from the shelter.

Welcome to Ottawa

As I was walking towards the welcoming area, I wondered if I had missed a step because I expected an immigration officer to stamp my passport or anything of the sort but no, everything had been done at the booth in Toronto. In my country, I witnessed a requirement for people to get their passports stamped. My general knowledge told me that this was the requirement. I was vigilant about not making mistakes. I thought that I did not want to be in my room just to see the police arrive to take me away. I asked a bystander whether I needed a stamp before I got out of the terminal and I was informed that it was all completed in Toronto. With that, I was comforted and ready to go.

As I exited the passenger terminal, I was welcomed by a taxi driver, and a very heavy blow of cold air, the kind that I had never felt on my skin before. I ran as fast as I could, into the taxi before I could even give the driver my address. At that point, I couldn't feel my fingers and toes. Yea, It was that bad. It was winter anyway, but that wasn't how cold I expected it to be. Coming from Africa where it is warm throughout the year, I knew I had bundled up very well in my jeans, long sleeve Tee, a knee length jacket, winter hat, gloves, and ankle-boots. I will confess that all these were not warm enough for the cold Canadian winter weather.

Making a Life

As we drove to my rented room, I couldn't help it but admire the beautifully lit roads. The snow also contributed to that beauty, and I couldn't stop looking in admiration.

People have their personal reasons for immigrating to another country. My choice was to experience the freedom including the freedom of new relationships that are not possible in my country. I wanted the ability to advance in life and career. The reasons for your immigration may not be comfortable saying aloud, but they are a truth that you must allow to warm your heart.

For a whole one week, I was indoors contemplating what I had to do next, and the cold weather couldn't easily let me explore the outside. The time inside allowed me to look inside myself. I could ask the questions about who I am and my goals. I could assess what strengths, interests, and skills I have.

I am not the same person I was when I arrived. I have grown tremendously. I desire to help others find their stride just as I have. What is truly important for me, and should be for you, is what is inside You. Seek to develop yourself. Prepare yourself. Build your skill. Fill your cup and you will have abundance to offer to others.

Section II: Living and Surviving

Chapter 3: Shelter

One week after, I checked in to a women shelter downtown Ottawa. The staff were very kind, welcomed me in, and they got me a futon bed to sleep on in the common area. I slept on the futon for two nights and I was blessed with a real bed on the third night in one of the shared bedrooms.

The following day, I set out to go to a public library which was in a ten minutes' walking distance. This turned out to be the longest distance I had ever walked in my entire life as the coldness had numbed my joints just midway the walk. At that point I had better winter wear, but the coldness was severe. I turned and practically ran back to the shelter. I did not give up on my visit to the library. I went again the following day, but this time I was more prepared.

On the fourth day, the social worker realised I had not paid for my stay at that women shelter. As a newcomer, I had no idea that I needed to pay to stay at that shelter though later I appreciated the fact that it was clean and organized, it meant that the residents were paying a certain fee for their stay.

The administration suggested that I moved out and directed me to a free shelter still in the downtown area. With my big suitcase, I hoped on to the city bus but clearly, I was not sure where I was going. I had been given a printout of the route to my new address, but I couldn't figure it out as it involved taking a bus and quite a long walk. I asked a lady next to me to help me interpret the directions the social worker had given me which she did, and she also showed me how to use the transit app on my smartphone for further guidance.

The Workers

The social workers are the people you engage with at first. They are your go-to people for guidance in almost every crucial starting point. They guide you into making that initial phone call to the city for allocation of financial resources and calling Legal Aid for a lawyer.

Social workers also help you find transportation routes, grocery stores, and other daily task-helping resources. The relationship you build is understandably personality based. The social workers know what a newcomer would want. That truly is the foundation of the relationship. It is truly transactional in many ways. Not very personal, but they will connect enough to know your specific needs in comparison to similar people. The social worker is your fall-back person.

Social workers, case workers, and immigration lawyers are all heroes in their own way, and they are paid by the government. The social workers were the ones who guided me to the other heroes. The city later assigns you a case worker to follow up on your social assistance. This is money given to you by the Government to cater for your needs monthly.

There is an Umbrella Body-Legal Aid Ontario which has member lawyers who you can choose from to represent you for free. They are paid by the Government for only a one-time legal representation. If you happen to fall out with your lawyer and you both terminate the contract before your immigration process is done, you need to hire one and they don't come cheap.

I managed to locate the second shelter and I checked in at about 7:00 PM. The social worker there told me they had run out of space, but she went ahead to say that she would find me a mat to sleep on the floor at the overflow area with other people in the soup kitchen. I also had to take care of my belongings.

My heart sank for a few minutes and tears rolled down my cheeks, as I was wondering how I was going to sleep on the mat, on the floor while having to guard my stuff. This was something that had never happened in my life. She went ahead to say that I had to come back later and check again with her which I did. She gave me the best news I had not expected. She had got me a bed in one of the rooms and I was to share it with another lady. I jumped in Thanksgiving and excitement.

How my roommate treated me for the time we shared the room, is a story for another time. I endured her longer than any of her former roommates. I found this out from one of the workers after I left. She was not kind. I will leave it at that.

Every morning by 9:30 AM the residents had to leave the premises and be back at 6:00 o'clock because the rooms had to be sanitized due to the outbreak of coronavirus. It didn't matter where one went, what you did, but we all had to be out of the building. I will say that the weather was not friendly for this kind of arrangement. I would go to the Public Library nearby to read, which I really loved. Other times I would go window shopping in the Rideau mall and the shops along the street. In between that, I had to go back to the soup kitchen for lunch which was always between 12:00 PM and

1:30 PM and dinner would be served between 5:30 PM and 7:00 PM. A few times I didn't make it in time for my meals and that meant that I had to go without food. I learned that keeping time (even for food) mattered a lot especially when I had no money to buy food somewhere else.

Submitting Your Claim

Some people prefer to "Give in" as soon as they exit the plane from their home country. Others enter inland and prepare their application for immigration. Filing a claim for residency is a process. As mentioned earlier there are people allocated to help throughout this process. My lawyer for example assisted me to organize my claim. He helped me put it together so that it was presentable and ready for submission. With the lawyer's help, you have a more polished claim than if you had prepared it yourself.

My experience at that shelter was another life learning experience because everything was surprisingly new and different, but I was grateful that I had a place to sleep, food to eat and a few sound-mind people to talk to.

It wasn't so long when the first lock down was passed, on March 16th, 2020. This meant that all public places would be closed. The shopping malls, public libraries, shops, cafes, were all closed. It became harder thereafter because I had nowhere to go to keep myself busy as the shelter policy of locking up the rooms throughout the day continued. I would wonder along the streets just to pass time. The weather by that time of the year was still a very big challenge as it was heavily snowing every day.

Time went by and on April 12th, 2020, I found www.stepstonehouse.ca which is a shelter/group home for newcomers and refugee claimants. I felt at home while living in that shelter. I could easily communicate with my fellow residents; we were allowed to prepare our special meals on top of what the house provided. We lived as one big happy family. The city would pay for my monthly rent there and gave me money for upkeep too. I am forever grateful for that. While in that house I volunteered my time to serve as a house manager. I enjoyed helping my fellow newcomers go through the settlement process as I was going through the same. This leadership position gave me opportunities for personal growth. I also volunteered as a coordinator between the shelter and iSisters www.iSisters.org , a non-for-profit organization pioneered by a group of brave women who empower other women especially newcomers by training them in information technology basics, navigating the job market, entrepreneurship, personal branding, and other life skills. My sincere gratitude goes to the executive director Ms. Ann McSweeney and her wonderful team for the opportunity which benefited me and my fellow newcomer women at the shelter.

I also used that time to sign up for a personal support worker program (PSW) as I waited for my work permit which I got later in March 2021. I started working immediately because I was looking forward to it. I got a job as a PSW/live-in caregiver. I was very honored to work for a very loving happy family, I understood what my clients' needs were, and I was determined to make them feel comfortable as much as I could. I felt happy and content working and living with this family. They made me feel at home too. Helping that senior couple felt like I was taking care of my parents (imagine having that kind of feeling on a job and you get paid at the same time, cool right? ☺ I was also blessed to have an amazing employer www.justlikefamily.ca

Chapter 4: Driving

By that time, I had got my G1 driving license which is part of the three stages of the Ontario Graduated Licensing program (G1, G2, and G). I wasn't an experienced driver back in my country of origin though I had a driver's license. Also, my country of origin wasn't listed as one of the countries with a driver's license exchange agreement with Canada so I couldn't apply for a Foreign Driver's License Exchange here in Ontario.

I could however still be eligible to use my years of driving experience from back home as a credit to skip part of the Ontario Graduated License Program. All in all, I chose to start afresh on a more confident ground which was rewarding.

By law, a G1 license holder is not supposed to drive alone on the roads but can do so with a co-driver who is fully licensed (full G-licence) and has driven for a minimum of 4 years. So, I would practice sometimes with my qualified friends which gave me more confidence on the road.

Driving School

Soon after that, I signed up with a local driving school and started studying for my G2 driving license. The theory part was longer and quite detailed though it was designed in a way that one would read it online at their own pace. At the end of each chapter were test questions which contributed to the overall pass mark.

Upon a successful completion of the theory part, I was set for the practical part. I remember my driving instructor asking me if I knew how to drive. My quick answer was a big 'yes' with a lot of confidence but that wasn't enough because he knew that most people said they knew how to drive but in actual sense they didn't.

During my first driving lesson with him, I realized that there were rules of the road that I didn't pay attention to while driving in my home country and yet they are seriously considered here in Canada by law. We have a unique situation on the roads in that part of the world where I came from. The roads are (if at all marked) marked differently, we drive on the left side, a few road signs and rules are in place, but the attitude of the drivers is different, a single lane road is shared amongst cars, tractors, trailers, motorcyclists, bicycle riders, pedestrians, and sometimes animals (I mean large herds of cattle).

I took it easy and learnt all that I was meant to learn and soon enough I was done with the whole course. I got a certificate of completion which I had to present when booking for a road test.

Road Test

I waited longer than expected for the road test appointment to come. This was so because the licensing authority had a big backlog of people waiting in the que due to COVID-19 virus.

My appointment date soon came, I went for the test and passed it. I was very excited; all I could think about was buying my car. I already knew the specific car I wanted and i always mentally saw it packed in the driveway. I just couldn't wait to buy it and see it in its physical form. I couldn't wait to surprise my friends, drive it to my appointments, it would be a big game changer in terms of saving time. The public transportation system here in Ottawa has not been very reliable. Most times some bus trips are skipped and that means that one must double the waiting time (30minutes or more). Imagine having to wait by the roadside for that long in winter. The train system also had operational issues on and off for a while, so people depended more on Uber/taxi services.

My New Car

It would be the first car that I bought and owned on my own. Back home, I would hire cars and drive, but did not have one on my own. I could not say that I could not afford a car, but I did not make it happen.

The thrill is what I remember as the first feeling. I still have that feeling. The driving school created the desire for me. The training in Canada ensures that you are fit to be on the road. Road infractions are serious. I prepared myself financially and psychologically. I was ready for this step.

I knew the brand, model, and color of the car I wanted. Arriving to the car sales lot, I saw lots of cars but surprisingly my car stood out and it was the only available car of its type. Due to Covid, cars were not readily available on the market. The few available ones were being sold expensively but that didn't hinder me from buying because it was a necessary need for me to have it.

It is an important experience and achievement for me. It is an example of the courage I am expressing in myself. I am growing into the consistency, discipline, and courage to go after what I want. The environment is making a difference as well. Here, the messages of progress and advancement are ever-present especially when you look for them.

Back home, I was a person that sought after what I wanted. The problem was that I was swimming against the tide of voices internally telling me that I was not good enough to go after what I want. Many of us have these self-limiting beliefs. The voices tell you that you are not knowledgeable, gifted, connected, or creative enough. They limit you by dampening your belief that you can do what you envision for yourself. Now, each achievement encourages me to work toward the next. The barriers decreased. The voices against me silenced. I work each day to increase my awareness of my ability, capacity, and brilliance. If the awareness is not there, you don't know what you are capable of. You languish in worry and fear foregoing the wonder and excitement of each opportunity. Succeed or fail, you learn. And therefore, you win.

I bought my car before I was even confirmed that I would legally stay in the country. I already believed 110% that I would be granted permanent residence to stay in Canada. I felt like this is where I belonged. I had no doubts about what would happen. I knew I was not going anywhere.

Section III: The Lessons to Send Back Home

Lastly, as I look back now, I realize that there were certain things that I did, and they helped me in my settlement journey. I am not yet fully settled in, but I am on the right course. I have mentioned some of them before and below I share more:

Chapter 6: Systems Knowledge

Knowledge of Place

Know your destination weather patterns. Oh yes, it pays off to do research about Canadian weather patterns. The months of December through March are usually the harshest in terms of coldness, so the right winter wear is absolutely the best idea. I wouldn't expose my body to severe coldness because it can be very serious leading to sickness.

Place is also about the institutions that you align with. I will discuss volunteerism as an action later, but the systems knowledge is crucial to your navigation and to your experience of happiness. I support you to develop a set of moral and ethical guidelines that can require your prosocial behavior.

Thankfully, I have not experienced inconsistencies in the place where I live. I have seen consistencies in the ways people define themselves and the way they operate. This may be because I am incessantly focused on the positive. And that's an important point about perception. Two people can look at the same thing and one perceive good, another perceives bad. What you bring to an event or an institution or a place makes a difference in what you perceive.

Trust in the system

Right from the beginning, by choice, I believed in the government system. It was an act of bravery and quite a bit of risk taking. I had thoughts that things were probably done differently in countries like Canada and indeed I later confirmed that thought. I set myself out to do whatever I was required to because of the trust I had in the system. I knew that the systems in place were there to help me reach my destination, not to fail me. I also liked the fact that there is a pool of opportunities and information resources open to everyone and if I tapped into that pool, I would improve my life.

Prior to coming to Canada, I did not have much planned out. I landed fresh. Before you sit with the immigration lawyer, you must prepare a story/narrative that is the Basis of Claim. A friend informed me ahead of time on what to say. The reason must be one that communicates the reasoning that you cannot go back to your country. You must evidence a true and present and reasonable fear of returning to your country.

You must understand the process. I came as a visitor. Others come as students. Your Basis of Claim is your announcement that you desire to seek conventional refugee status in the host country. Later, you must produce evidence to back up your claim. I knew nothing of this as I sat in front of the immigration lawyer. You must know that the story will be necessary. Remember that you must show evidence later.

It is a process toward a hearing for conventional refugee status. You don't know when you will have that hearing.

Your lawyer has put together the claim and submitted it. Later your notice to appear for hearing will come within 1-3 months to the set hearing date. If you feel like you still have more pieces of evidence to present, you are still free to do so. You must present this information to the lawyer, and they send it to the immigration office. After having the hearing, you will be notified of the decision after a time of deliberation by the judge. They tell you what you are accepted into the country as or whether you are rejected or requested to provide more evidence (Of course, this is stressful).

Dissimilarity from Back Home

People in this country are free to express themselves. In my country, people may do many things, but they do it in hiding. There was a time when my parliament debated the question of sexual orientation as a protected decision. Parents, churches, and many in government were against any protected status allowing or encouraging homosexuality to be in the open. The discussions included debates about the origin of homosexuality. The supportive arguments sought to accept people because they were born this way. The opposition rejected that argument stating that it was social engineering at work.

Here in Canada, you will see many things occur out in the open that could be surprising. Even years after my arrival, I am still a product of my socialization. I have visited a few countries around the world, and I must say that the expression and openness is much more open here. I have never been inconvenienced or wronged by people who have obviously adopted a lifestyle that could be described in the LGBTQ space. I see people daily who are same sex holding hands or showing public affection. The rainbow festivals and parades are commonplace and accepted widely.

Back home, I did not get a chance to see expression of alternative lifestyles. I feel like I accepted people for who they are, what they have gone through, and how they chose to live their lives. I also would have thought that some event is the origin of their decision making and expression. Yet, that is not a proper acceptance or understanding.

The opportunity is to look at people from the standpoint of their humanness rather than judging them or distancing yourself from them. See people with the same eyes you see everyone. Mind your business and accept that you do not know what is going on in their world. Of course, I am curious and wonder about their journeys, but I have no malice. That is the pattern to follow. You don't need to feel anything different for one human versus another. Every human is free to express themselves, including you.

I was so afraid of being judged. That made me more judgmental. I am now accepting that I make mistakes. I am more aware. I accept that other people have a level of awareness that offers certain choices for them. It is not my duty to judge others or control them just like it is not their place to judge me. Now, I am more accepting of myself, which translates into greater acceptance of others. If this is you, and it probably is, work toward accepting yourself and freeing yourself. You will learn to accept others in the process.

Chapter 7: Mental Habits

Positive Attitude

My take on this has always been to focus on the good in everything. Let's face it, life is not a bed of roses; how I choose to look at a situation however challenging it may be, is entirely up to me. I conditioned myself to look at the positives because I knew what I wanted and keeping myself in that positive mindset gave me the boost that I always needed to move forward.

Have a dream for your future. Everyone has that overall big reason behind their need to relocate. Think through it with clarity and always have it at heart. Some may question how you can be in a situation of survival, but also maintain a dream. It may be personal, but you can cultivate it.

I never give up. My friends know me for this. I know that the situation is not the end. It will pass. I have hope and I will keep going to engage that hoped for reality. I knew if I could just set foot into Canada, I could find the foundation for all the dreams I had.

I wanted to experience these joys. Nothing could stop me. Nothing.

Open Mind

This is one of the traits that I learnt along the way whereby I developed the willingness to consider new ideas. At some point I also realised that some of my old ideas and habits were not serving me well, so I trained myself to adjust to new ones. This gave me the ability to grow as a person and learn so much about the world around me.

Like a person who has been in prison for 30 years, living in a new environment can be difficult. Consider that the journey of accepting the pathway in front of you is critical. As you see where you are and where you want to be in your life, trust that continuing intentionally will get you where you want to be eventually.

Decisiveness

My ability to make my own decisions put me in a better position. Sometimes there would be a lot of information flowing in from all corners, people advising me to do things in a certain way, but I always knew that if something never resonated with me or my values, I wouldn't even try it. It is good to get different opinions about an issue, but I always trusted my intuition when deciding (occasionally the decisions made may not necessarily be the best but at least I would learn to think better next time).

I think of this as being realistic about your goals. You will have grand dreams that take time to accomplish. You do not need to disregard your aspirations to drive a Rolls Royce, but you must make that realistic in terms of time. The right action steps towards your goals and the continuous anticipation will lead you there. You can always start by utilizing what you have available to you, like your talents.

Continuous anticipation describes an attraction you maintain. Remain open to new resources and help. You will find that the resources and help come when you maintain a posture of expectation. When those opportunities arise, you must address them with decisiveness and without hesitation. Employ the specific actions including what you need to prepare yourself for. The preparation phase reinforces the anticipation. You are ready when the opportunities come because you expect them AND prepare for them.

Chapter 8: Behavioral Habits

Persistence

The one thing that I have always held with a lot of Faith is the result of my journey. My whole journey is founded upon persistence. Some people gave up and went back to their home countries because the challenges are real. I made up my mind that I was not going back. I knew where I wanted to be. Nothing could stop me from living my dream.

Being in a new environment and everything around me seemingly new, I had no option but to employ my ability to keep a firm grip on the course of my journey despite difficulty here and there while focusing on my big picture. It was more than what I was leaving behind. My persistence was about what I was making possible by being in this new space.

Patience

I can't stress this enough. When going through the refugee claimant process, COVID-19 hit, this brought about long delays, I had no control over the whole process. I had to exercise patience of the highest degree during that time when nothing seemed moving, otherwise sometimes I would get feelings of giving up, but I always brought back my awareness to the reasons why I boarded that plane to come here. I often contemplated all the reasons that I had immigrated. I reflected upon my desires to create a life for myself and my future.

The long wait without information is the first task even beyond the living, eating, and weather challenges. All I could do was wait. There were delays caused by COVID-19 but that didn't put me off track, I in fact utilized that waiting time to do constructive things as already shared. I studied online courses that I only later realized prepared me for my work permit and first employment.

Adaptability

This is my other strength in life. My ability to adjust to new conditions by exhibiting elastic-like energy and a willingness to face challenges whenever my circumstances change has greatly helped me along my journey. People often say to me that, "Even if you are thrown into a desert, you will thrive." That is true about me. I have accepted it.

I was raised by my grandmother. She would always take me from place to place. I had to interact in different environments with various people, of course these were good people. The result is that I became astute at observing behavior and fitting in adaptable to the environment I found myself in.

You must give yourself permission to adjust to new environments. Resist the fear. Fear is based on rigid expectations about the new environment. Instead, enter with an open mind and the expectation that everything is going to work out. Regardless of what happens or the difficulties in the environment, you will exercise your trust that everything will work out. You are flexible and adaptable enough to make it happen.

Chapter 9: Learning Orientation

Curiosity

Learning opportunities are everywhere. Whenever I thought of opportunities, study has always come first. Free online courses came in handy (there is free Wi-Fi almost everywhere we live). I utilised the waiting time to study/learn something new.

During the lock-down and physical distancing requirement worldwide, I utilized the time to engage with content and students online. The most vibrant experience is inside of a classroom. That's what I enjoy. The certificate was in personal support work. I chose it because it is a position in high demand. It is also a short course with a secure work opportunity at the end of the training.

Curiosity is interest backed by your goals. I wanted to earn money the best way I could. That goal, time available, and interest combined to move me to action even though online courses are not my favorite. I also strategized that the timing would set me up for opportunities once my work permit was available for me.

Volunteerism

I chose to involve myself in volunteer work as a way of serving others. I volunteered as a house manager in the third shelter I stayed in. All the residents were from Africa. We shared a history and cultural aspects like food. I also coordinated a training for women with a Non-Government Organization (NGO) connected to the house. I trained in computer use and job market skills.

In the process, I developed many of my skills especially leadership skills, I also grew as a person. I later realized that volunteer work is considered as part of work experience here in Canada. One might get involved to keep themselves busy with something constructive. Your sharing of expertise can be a great contribution to those around you.

Support

A good support team meant a lot to me. I carefully chose the kind of people I associated myself with and from these people I built myself a strong 'support team'. A little encouragement here and there, wise counsel, and so many other things that I wouldn't be able to do by myself, like where to buy personal items, where to go if I needed resources from the government, these people were always there to help me. I am forever grateful to them.

The workers, especially the caseworker, was a great support for me. I have heard stories about people who have not had great experiences, but my experience was all positive. The women in the third shelter were also a great support. The shared culture in the context of a new culture was invaluable for peace of mind. The owner of the shelter was a Ugandan. It was community to me.

Chapter 10: Self-Sufficiency

Self-Support

I would like to say that being my number one cheerleader, I have always pushed myself and created that energy and resilience. This always worked as the fuel to keep me moving in the right direction.

Sometimes life is a challenge. I realize that I have multiple priorities. In addition to the progress, I want to make personally, and, in my career, I want to connect with my people back home. For me, self-support comes from priority setting.

The priority is my job because that pays the bills, but that is not the most important thing. Money is critical because the money freedom supports the time freedom. I can travel when I have the money. When you have money, you can employ other people to help or to do things that you find challenging.

I must make time for the most things that provide me with joy and satisfaction. I manage my activities to fit within the available time, but I also ensure that I make time intentionally for enjoyment. This highlights the personal aspects of life.

My awareness is heightened as I am getting older. Body, mind, soul, and social are vital aspects of life that you must engage continually. I select activities to stimulate each of those areas and grow as a person. The outcome is directly related to the goal: Being my best self is found in giving of myself. The more I give, the more I get.

Love for Myself

Being kind and compassionate to myself. It is a sweet simple reminder to be kind, tender and compassionate to oneself. Some days may be brighter than others, things may not work out as expected during a given time but knowing that I did what I was meant to do, left me with no option but to simply breathe and let the tide pass as I knew that everything would be working out for my highest good.

We are all different and love ourselves in unique ways. For me, I begin the night before to set up my experience for the next day. The first concern is to have a restful sleep. I rehearse my gratitude prior to bed. I sleep within that positive space.

The next day has the foundation of the night before. I wake and engage exercises in my space. I enter meditation. I state my gratitude again for what I am thankful for. I continue throughout the day giving myself grace and prioritizing myself. It is not about selfishness, but it is about checking with myself first.

Celebration

Reward yourself. By rewarding yourself, I mean part yourself on the back, give yourself credit for any effort and action taken towards achieving something good, big, or small. I would give myself a special treat for example take myself out for dinners, buy myself something nice if I can afford it, buy myself flowers because I love them ☺ , go for a massage or even simply putting myself in that winners' feeling is a great feeling in itself and it helps build more confidence. I never had to wait for somebody to tell me 'You did well.'

You may not have people in your life that give you positive reinforcement. I give myself credit for what I have accomplished and what I am working on. My responsibility to myself is to find the moments of celebration that make a life. It is one thing to arrive, it is quite another to thrive.

Mindfulness

Enjoy the journey. Lastly, it was very important for me to live in the moment. I would try to make my days fun and enjoyable by taking walks in the neighbourhood or parks, listening to music, jogging (I found jogging partners in the area), cooking, and many other activities that bring joy to me (find out what works for you). I would be looking forward to each new day with anticipation of something good coming my way. The end goal is worth the work, but I also wanted to make the journey worth remembering in a good way.

> Success is not final,
> Failure is not fatal,
> It is the courage to continue that counts.
> -Winston S. Churchill

Olivia R. Nansubuga

www.ingramcontent.com/pod-product-compliance
Lightning Source LLC
Chambersburg PA
CBHW072015060426
42446CB00043B/2562